SAFARI LIVING

First published in the United Kingdom in 2006 by Scriptum Editions
an imprint of Co & Bear Productions (UK) Ltd
Copyright © 2006 Co & Bear Productions (UK) Ltd
Photographs copyright © 2006 Tim Beddow

ISBN-10 1 902 686 56 X
ISBN-13 978 1 902 686 56 1

Publisher Beatrice Vincenzini & Francesco Venturi
Executive Director David Shannon
Design Brian Rust

First edition
1 3 5 7 9 10 8 6 4 2

Printed in Italy

SAFARI LIVING

PHOTOGRAPHY BY TIM BEDDOW

SCRIPTUM EDITIONS

BY THE TURN OF THE NINETEENTH CENTURY, Europe had "discovered" Africa. The European powers were awakened to the potential of the vast continent by pioneering explorers who ventured into the interior for the first time. Britain's Royal Geographical Society sponsored a number of early expeditions to Africa, including those of John Speke and Dr. David Livingstone to find the source of the Nile River (eventually traced to Lake Victoria), and that of Sir Harry Johnston to survey Mount Kilimanjaro.

More than a century after the first safari expedition brought Europeans into direct contact with the wilds of Africa, out of pleasure rather than necessity, the lure of the experience endures. Moreover, the imagery associated with the safari has in itself come to be symbolic of something more: The flickering of a hurricane lamp casting shadows against the canvas walls of a tent; soft swathes of fine mosquito netting shrouding a camp bed; a folding table set with white linen and silverware in the shade of a solitary flame tree; vast stretches of savannah turning gold in the evening sun; the pattern of zebra moving together on the horizon; and the warm glow of a campfire, beyond which the bush resonates with the language of wildlife. The travelers who captured these images, through their snapshots and writings, evoked a life of both pleasure and adventure, of elemental living in an extraordinary place.

Africa was the adventure playground of wealthy and eccentric Europeans, who came to see for themselves the wild beauty, unbounded spaces, and cultural exoticism of this great continent – it later became their home ...

COTTAR CAMP, a four-hour drive south of Nairobi, sits in an exclusive concession of 100,000 acres at Olentoro, in one of the satellite ranches of the Masai Mara Game Reserve.

7

THE TERRACED LEVELS offers views over the plains of Nairobi National Park with its roaming herds of giraffe, zebra, ostrich, and wildebeest. Keeping watch from the roof is a contemporary statue of a warrior from the *Acholi* tribe in Uganda, created by African Heritage artist John Adochameny.

ON THE SHORES of lake Naivasha, the grand English tradition of building follies continues. The eight-storied tower soars 115 feet into the treetops.

THOUGHT TO be the first in the district to be built in stone – this colonial style bungalow, built in 1904, was designed to evoke the coziness of a traditional English country cottage.

12

BORANA LODGE blends perfectly with the surrounding countryside, high in the northern frontier district of Kenya. The surrounding hills are wooded, but the valley below is fairly dry with whistling thorns, acacia trees, scrub, and some open grassland.

A SHADY COURTYARD is characterized by thick white supporting columns. This architectural device is typical of the Arab world, which is not only decorative but helps to soften the harsh African sun.

17

THE LODGES at Ngorongoro Crater Lodge are made almost entirely from wood – from plantations rather than wild forests – and mud brick. The roofs are made from palm fronds, lined with banana leaves.

A MAGICAL COMBINATION of
Arab exoticism and colonial grandeur,
The Serena Inn is situated on the
waterfront at the edge of Stone Town,
overlooking the Indian Ocean. Dhows,
identical in style to those navigated
by Arab traders along the Spice route
last century, still sail the waters
around Zanzibar.

NAMED "OSERIAN" ("place of
peace" in the Masai language), its tranquil
appearance now belies the boisterous
scenes once played out here by the
colourful characters of the Happy Valley
set. The minaret and dome are more
in keeping with mosque architecture.

SIMPLE, WHITE-WASHED walls, and Arab influenced, wooden furniture make this coastal retreat a tranquil haven.

31

A **BEAUTIFULLY SIMPLE**, Arab-style mansion, with spacious living areas and an internal courtyard. Bright whitewashed walls, structural details in African hardwoods, Moorish windows and colonnade, limewashed walls and sprinkling of palms and a lily pond complete the picture.

THE CEDAR VERANDAS that edge the house upstairs and downstairs provide a perfect vanatge point from which to spot widlife. More than 250 bird species nest among the dense forest of acacia, olive and fig trees.

THE HUTS ARE built from natural materials such as palm leaves and local wood. Bold fabric stripes create a colorful border around windows, doors, and around the walls. The gap between the walls and roof allows air to circulate freely.

TWENTY FEET OFF the ground, the views, over the thick bushland with its abundant wildlife, are wonderful. The treehouses, that took a year and a half build, feature an ingenious entrance hatch which closes automatically with the help of attached weights.

43

THE ULTIMATE LUXURY on a hot African day: a collection of
swimming pools in which to relax and cool off after a hard
days exploring – hippos not allowed.

A **BREATHTAKING** view from an infinity pool, perched on an African hillside.

COOL AND SERENE, the main living area of Mnemba Island Lodge creates an informal mood. The colour scheme echoes the outside view of a white sandy beach, translucent water, and brilliant blue sky.

THE ROOFTOP TERRACE has an exotic Arab-Swahili character, with a Zanzibari menu served under a canopied roof. Guests unwind on giant appliquéd pillows to watch the sun setting over Stone Town. As the light fades, candles are lit in traditional brass lanterns.

THIS POOL HOUSE is thatched with *makuti* palm leaves, typical of roofing along Africa's eastern coast. Hanging from the ceiling are three pendant lamps fashioned out of traditional fish traps from Kenya and Madagascar. The long sofa is covered with a tribal fabric from Mali called *bokolofino*.

53

STAIRS LEAD UP through the central courtyard of
the house to the terrace on the first floor, where a
mass of bougainvillea offers shade and color.
Household life tends to focus on this open-air
living area, which provides padded banquettes for
relaxing, and a dining table and chairs made by
Lamu woodworkers.

THE GROUND-FLOOR level with its elaborately carved plasterwork, once contained the harem. It looks out onto a central courtyard, where a single palm grows up through the house.

THE VERANDA is seventy-two feet long, providing ample room for separate outdoor dining and living areas, perfect for afternoon naps or entertaining.

THE MOORISH INFLUENCE can be felt in these shady courtyards with their whitewashed colonades and colourful tiles impoerted from Spain.

THE THATCHED COTTAGES are designed so that the views can be enjoyed while lying in bed. The cottages look directly out onto a forest of acacia tortillas, with open savanna and the volcanic peak of Mount Kilimanjaro in the distance

THE VIEWING PLATFORM and sundeck of the Rhino Suite overlook the Galana River and Yatta Escarpment. This secluded vantage point is ideal for observing the rhinos and buffalos that cluster around the river in the early morning and evening, or simply for enjoying a glass of wine and plate of ripe mango.

AN ELEVATED VERANDA runs along the front of the house, and is often used as a dining area for breakfast and lunch. Wicker-backed planters chairs and a sofa provide seating for evening drinks.

THIS PRISTINE kitchen looks
pristine with its white-washed
walls and scrubbed wood benches.
There are no extraneous details,
and everything in the room has
a practical purpose, in line with
the owner's belief that a vacation
home should be kept free of
distractions, and be as easy as
possible to maintain.

THE EXOTIC BED that dominates the room belonged to a wealthy merchant in the 1930s. Its unusual construction, with netting suspended from a frame, is designed to accommodate a ceiling fan.

EACH TENT is furnished in a manner befitting royalty. Polished four-poster beds are made up with crisp white cotton sheets and handmade quilts filled with ostrich feathers. The covered porch is set with canvas-slung rocking chairs and a small table where afternoon tea is served.

TAKING PRIDE of place in the tent is an eight-foot bed made from Burmese teak. The precious wood came from a boat carrying a cargo of tea, which was wrecked off the Kenyan coast.

DINNER IS SERVED in the open mess tent, or under the stars on especially warm nights. The table is set with antique china, crystal glasses, and silver cutlery. Other authentic details include a 1920s gramophone and brass hurricane lamps.

THE BATHROOM is a zipped compartment within the tent. Although there is no running water, facilities are far from primitive. The bath, a canvas sling on a folding wooden frame, is filled with hot water on request. A porcelain sink, handmade toweling robes, and mahogany toilet seat are unexpected finds.

THE BANDA sits on a floor of plantation-grown cypress, with tented walls and a thatched roof. As with a tent, the front canvas flap is zipped up at night but opens during the day onto a sun-drenched veranda with views of the river. Most of the furnishings are fashioned from stone and wood found around the camp.

THE AFRICAN SUN gives the stone walls and natural wood furnishing in this bedroom a cosy, natural warmth.

WATER SPORTS on Mnemba Island take many forms. As the island has never been settled, used only by fishermen as a haven from storms, the beaches are completely unspoiled. Guests need to stray no further than water's edge, beachcombing for beautiful shells, or simply drinking in the view.

THE ROOF ON this lodge are made from reed thatch, which is twisted around fine cedar sticks to give an interesting knotted effect from the inside and a typical thatched look from the outside.

THIS LIVING AREA features a wall of full-length windows, repeated above on the gallery level. The room has been kept intentionally free of color, allowing the greens of the garden to filter through instead. The window surrounds throughout the house are stone-dressed using an old English technique.

THE CEILINGS are constructed using durable mangrove poles.
The walls are built of coral blocks up to half a meter thick. Door and
window frames are made from bomba kofi, an exotic hardwood.

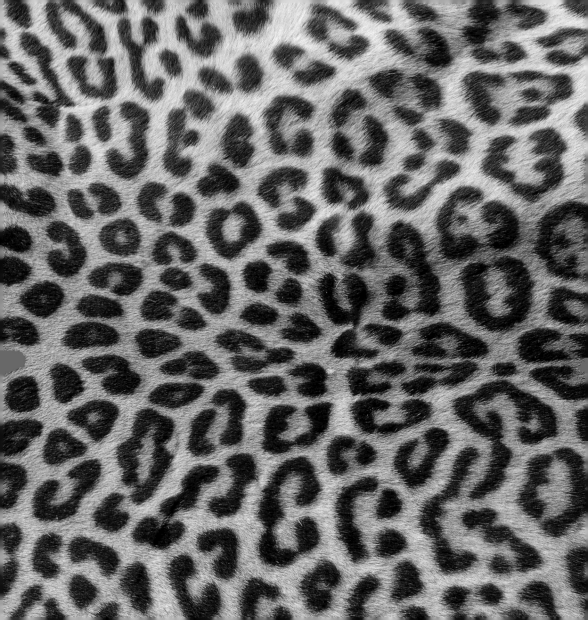

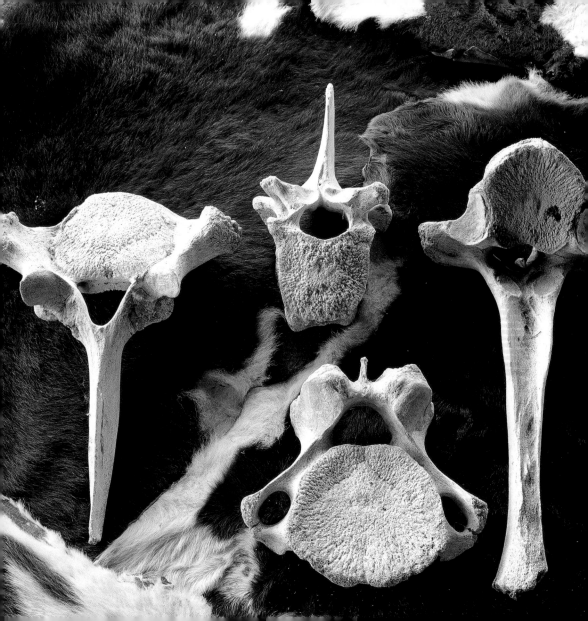

AN INTRICATELY carved Indian screen serves as a backdrop for a display of African and Indian textiles. On the wall is a circumcision mask of brass appliqué on wood – it is worn by boys of the Marka tribe in Mali.

A **ROOFTOP** sitting room featuring wall decoration based on a Masai shield design. The sofa and cushions are covered in Mali mud cloth. Intricately embroidered *Bakuba* cloth trails over a four-poster bed from Lamu.

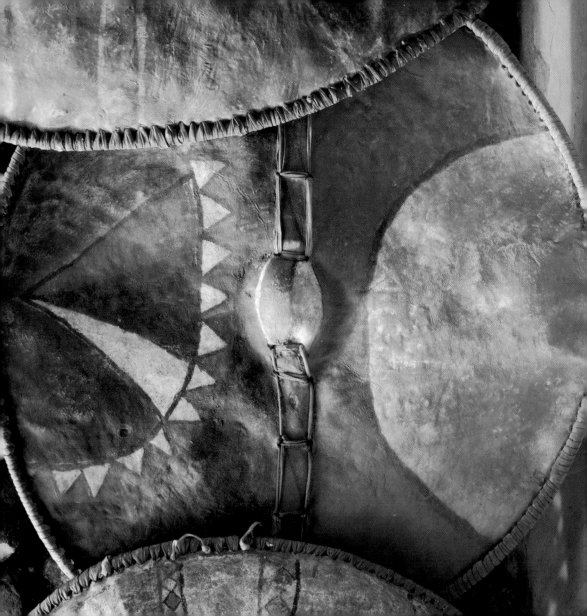

IN EACH TREEHOUSE, a niche above the stairway is converted into a seating area, complete with sofa, for reclining, reading, or simply admiring the view.

THIS ORGANIC COMPLEX of wood, earth and leaves, seems to have almost grown out of the surrounding bushland.

THE BANISTERS are made from timber reclaimed from demolition sites around Mombasa, while the sofa is fashioned from an antique bedhead carved by the bajuni artisans on the island of Lamu.

TONIO TRZEBINSKI makes furniture, art, and sculpture to sell, as well as for his own houuse. Common to all his creations is a strong sense of wild Africa, and many of his materials are gathered from the bush.

111

THE "MESS", surving as both dining and lounge area, is an impressive textural mix of natural elements and native art. The floor is paved with natural stone slabs from Mombasa, and the roof is thatched with coconut palm leaves.

BOTH THE SOFA and dining table were made at the lodge from fallen olive trees, and the upholstery and cushions are in hand-painted fabric from Zimbabwe.

A COLLECTION of doors illustrating the Arab and Indian influences that can be seen in architectural details throughout East Africa.

THE GRAPHIC NATURE of African arts and crafts is used to dramatic effect in the living room. The double-sided sofa in the center of the room is made from a baby cradle from Lamu, and is covered with Mali mud cloth.

LIKE MANY PERMANENT lodges in Africa, this sturdy dwelling is made from local, timber and local stone. The fireplace is proof that, even Africa, has its cooler seasons.

SPACIOUS OPEN-PLAN, sitting-cum-dining rooms are a common feature of many safari lodges, and provide the focal point for camp life.

THE COLOURFUL WALLS and ceilings are hand-painted with designs based on the geometric patterns of mud cloth from Mali.

131

A VISION OF contrasts: lavish European and raw native elements collide in this dining room. The polished floors are of mnenga wood, the ceilings and crystal chandeliers were made by local, Masai artisans.

132

ORNATE, HAND-CARVED, glazed doors, with unusual wrought-iron fixtures, frame breathtaking views over the forest below.

RAISED OFF the ground on wooden posts, these simple, thatched tents provide all the comfort and shelter needed on safari.

136

A **SINGLE, LARGE** mosquito net, suspended from the crossbeams, provides ample protection for a pair of simple beds.

THE JEWEL COLORS, rich Indian silks, and
ornately carved furnishings in this bedroom
conjure up images of the Arab Sultans that
ruled Zanzibar in the eighteenth century.

PERCHED ON its banks, this open-fronted lodge affords views out across the Rufiji river. The traditional canoe is, now, only for decorative purposes.

A CAVERNOUS OPEN-SIDED lodge, with polished stone floors, serves
as dining room, meeting room, lounge and possibly nightclub for
the whole camp.

SUEDE BEDCOVERS and silk organza cushions create a sense of decadent luxury, in sharp contrast with native African elements such as the clutch of Masai spears displayed in one corner of the room.

THIS COTTAGE is a showcase for the work of local artists. Fabrics and textiles have been sourced from all over Kenya, and are sewn up on-site by an old tailor with an ancient sewing machine.

BEDS WITHOUT tall posts, will have cotton nets cascading from custom-made canopies above the headboards.

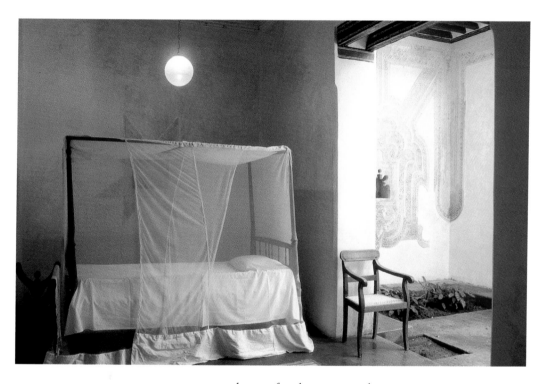

THE EVER-PRESENT threat of malaria means that almost all bedrooms will have a four-poster bed shrouded in fabric.

A BEDROOM SUITE recreates the feel of a Swahili harem, with the bed enclosed by curtains of sheer muslin netting.

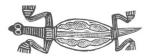

THESE KING-SIZED beds, and most other furnishings, are made from local woods found in the area and are draped romantically in cotton mosquito nets of different colours.

AS NIGHT FALLS, a table is laid out on the lagoon shores, illuminated by torch flames and hurricane lamps, and setting the scene for an evening feast under the stars.

THE BATHROOMS are decorated with molded plaster panels, hand finished by artists on-site. They include a mix of antique and reproduction pieces, as well as ethnic African objects.

ROUGH BUSH TEXTURES give the bathroom a primitive feel. The stone basin is set into a stack of river rocks, and solar-powered lamps are made from Ostrich eggshells fixed on buffalo vertebrae.

THE HIGH CEILING in the lounge area is lined with hundreds of banana leaves folded over a wire frame, and supports a crystal chandelier. The paneled walls were created by a team of fifty carpenters and carvers from Zanzibar.

THE WALLS are made from chunks of orangey sandstone cemented together with a mixture that includes the deep red soil of the valley. The overall effect is earthy, warm and comforting.

167